Augustus Schultze

The Books of the Bible

Augustus Schultze

The Books of the Bible

ISBN/EAN: 9783742809766

Manufactured in Europe, USA, Canada, Australia, Japa

Cover: Foto ©Lupo / pixelio.de

Manufactured and distributed by brebook publishing software
(www.brebook.com)

Augustus Schultze

The Books of the Bible

THE

BOOKS OF THE BIBLE

BRIEFLY ANALYZED,

FOR USE IN

BIBLE INSTRUCTION AND FOR BIBLE
STUDENTS IN GENERAL,

BY

A. SCHULTZE,

President Moravian Theological Seminary.

THIRD EDITION.
REVISED AND CORRECTED.

EASTON, PA.:
H. T. FRUEAUFF.
1890.

PREFACE.

THIS publication has been prepared for the purpose of furnishing the Bible Student with a comprehensive view of the contents of the various books contained in the Holy Scriptures, and of facilitating the study of the Word of God. May it stimulate the reader to search the Book of books, which is able to make wise unto salvation, through faith in Christ Jesus our Lord.

A. SCHULTZE.

BETHLEHEM, PA.

THE BIBLE

is divided into two principal parts, the *Old* and
the *New Testaments*, the former comprising the
books that were written before the birth of our
Saviour, the latter embracing the writings that
were composed after that event.   The Old Testament contains thirty-nine books and the New
twenty-seven, making sixty-six in all.   The *books*
of the Old Testament were formerly divided, for
the convenience of reading, into sections called
Parshioth or Haphtaroth, and those of the New
Testament into Lectionaries or church-lessons.
Since the thirteenth century of the Christian era
the present division into chapters has come into
general use.

A.—THE OLD TESTAMENT.

The Jewish church divided the books of the Old
Testament into three classes, viz.: the Torah or the
Law, the Nebiim or the Prophets and the Ketubim or the Holy Writings.   The Torah contained
the Pentateuch, that is the first five books of the
Bible; the Ketubim comprised the Psalms, Proverbs, Job, Ecclesiastes, the Song of Solomon,
Ruth, Chronicles, Ezra, Nehemiah, Esther, Lamen-
tations and Daniel; the Nebiim included the remaining books.   The Christian church divides
the 39 books of the Old Testament into 17
historical, 17 prophetical and 5 poetical or
doctrinal books.

I.—HISTORICAL BOOKS.

The historical books of the Old Testament contain the history of the "ancient covenant" between God and mankind, particularly of the covenant between God and the people of Israel, and date from the creation of Adam to the reformation of Nehemiah, that is from about 4000–400 B. C.

1.—Genesis.

The book called Genesis (origin of historical events) includes the history from Adam till the death of Joseph, the date of the latter event being variously fixed between the years 1850 and 1600 B. C. The earlier portion of the book, to the end of the eleventh chapter, is a religious history of the ancient world, and the latter portion, a history of the fathers of the Hebrew race. Genesis has 50 chapters which, for the sake of symmetry, may be arranged in four groups, each containing 12 chapters, with the last two chapters as an appendix; *viz.*:

Chapters 1–12, the *world's* history from *Adam* to *Abraham;* 1–6, from Adam to Noah and to the deluge; 7–12, from Noah to Abraham.
" 13–24, the *history of Abraham* (and Isaac).
" 25–36, the *history of Jacob.*
" 37–48, the *history of Joseph.*

Chapters 49 and 50 add the "blessing" of Jacob and his death, and the death of Joseph.

2.—Exodus.

The book of Exodus (*i. e.*, Departure) describes the bondage of the children of Israel in Egypt, their deliverance and their migration from Egypt to Mount Sinai; it also contains the promulgation of the law from Mount Sinai and the erection of the tabernacle. The date of the Exodus is uncertain, but is placed by many writers at 1492 B. C. The book has 40 chapters which are divided into two very nearly equal parts, the first historical, the second legislative, *viz.:*

Chapters 1-19, the *historical part*, which may be subdivided; 1-6, Israel's bondage and the calling of Moses; 7-12, the ten plagues and the exodus; 13-19, the migration from Egypt to Sinai.

" 20-40, the *legislative part;* 20-24, the first promulgation of the law; 25-31, the plan of the tabernacle, and order of worship; 32-34, the sin of the people and the renewal of the covenant; 35-40, the building of the tabernacle.

3.—Leviticus.

The book called Leviticus, *i.e.*, levitical precepts, contains a fuller account of the Mosaic Law, mainly of the ceremonial law and of ordinances relating to the Levites and priests. The order followed, while not strictly systematical, shows a certain plan, which may be outlined by grouping the 27 chapters of the book in three divisions of about 9 chapters each; *viz.:*

Chapters 1-10, the *laws relating to sacrifices and the priesthood.* 1-7, the sacrifices; 8-10 the priesthood.

" 11-20, the *laws* concerning *purity* and impurity; 11-16, clean and unclean; 17-20 Israel separated from the heathen.

" 21-27, the *laws* concerning *holy orders* and *holy seasons.*

4.—Numbers.

This book takes its name from the double numbering or census of the people, the first of which is given in chapters 1-4, and the second in chapter 26. It embraces the history of the march of the Israelites through the desert, from the time of their leaving Sinai until their arrival at the borders of the promised land, together with the special laws given during this period. If the date of the exodus as given before is correct, the period here comprised would be 1490–1450 B. C.

Numbers is divided into 36 chapters, which may be arranged in three groups, *viz:*

Chapters 1-9, *the host of Israel,* or preparations for the departure; especially levitical appointments,

" 10-19, the journey *to Kadesh* and the *wanderings* in the wilderness, 10 14, from Sinai to Kadesh; 15-19, the wanderings.

" 20-36, the journey *from Kadesh to the east side of the Jordan;* 20-25, from Kadesh to the plains of Moab; 26-30, special legislation; 31-36, on the east side of Jordan; additional laws.

5. —Deuteronomy.

Deuteronomy signifies a "repetition of the law." This title expresses the general scope of the book, which is a review of the forty years in the wilderness, including the laws which had been given. It consists of three discourses delivered by Moses, shortly before his departure, and closes with the story of his death. Hence the 34 chapters of Deuteronomy arrange themselves, as follows:

First discourse, chapters 1–4, recapitulation of the *history* of the forty years.

Second " " 5–26, recapitulation of the *Sinaitic law.*

Third " " 27–33, the solemn charge, or *blessings* and *curses*

Chapter 34 contains an account of the death of Moses. The second discourse, which recapitulates the enactments of the law, may be subdivided into four groups, *viz:*

Chapters 5–11, the moral law.

" 12–16, the ceremonial law.

" 17–21, the laws relating to government.

" 22–26, the laws relating to social life.

6.—Joshua.

The book of Joshua sets forth the acts of Joshua, in connection with the conquest and the division of the land of Canaan, comprising a period of about 30 years, possibly 1450–1420 B. C. It has 24 chapters which divide themselves, naturally, into two equal parts, *viz:*

Chapters 1–12, *the conquest of Canaan ;* 1–5, preparations for, and the passage of the Jordan ; 6–10, the conquest of the South ; 11–12, the conquest of the North.

" 13–24, *the division of Canaan,* and Joshua's farewell ; 13–22, assigning of territories ; 23–24, the last days of Joshua.

7.—Judges.

In this book are recorded the achievements of a number of leaders, who arose in the Hebrew republic to deliver their countrymen from the

oppressions of neighboring nations. The period
comprised in this book includes the time from
the death of Joshua to the death of Samson,
that is from about 1400-1100 B. C. It has 21
chapters, divided as follows :

Chapters 1-16,*the history of this period;* 1-5,from
Joshua till Deborah ; 6-9, Gideon
and his family ; 10-12, Jephthah ;
13-16, Samson.
" 17-21, *an appendix* containing two epi-
sodes from the times of the Judges

8.—Ruth.

The book of Ruth was, originally, a part of the
book of Judges, and is a supplement to that book,
while at the same time, it serves as an introduction to the history of David. Its four chapters
narrate the history of faithful Ruth, the ances-
tress of King David.

Chapters 1-2, Ruth coming to Bethlehem.
" 3-4, her marriage with Boaz.

9.—Samuel.

The two books of Samuel, in the original
Hebrew Canon, formed but one book. They take
their name from Samuel, the last judge and the
founder of the schools of the prophets, who played
a prominent part during the first portion of that
period.

I Samuel records the history of the lives and
times of the prophet Samuel and of King Saul,
about 1100-1050 B. C. The 31 chapters of this
book may be divided as follows :

Chapters 1-8, *the high priest Eli and the prophet
Samuel;* 1-4, Eli ; 5-8, Samuel.
" 9-15, *King Saul chosen and rejected;* 9-12.
Saul's election ; 13-15, his wars.

" 16-31, *Saul's reign, and his enmity against David;* 16-26, David at Saul's court and persecuted by him ; 27-31, David sojourning with the Philistines.

10.—II Samuel.

The second book of Samuel contains the history of King David, after the death of Saul, that is the period from about 1050 to 1000 B. C. It is divided into 24 chapters which may be arranged in three groups, as follows :

Chapters 1-10, *David's glorious reign* at Hebron and in Jerusalem ; 1-4, at Hebron ; 5-10, at Jerusalem.
" 11-20, *David's sin and the rebellion of Absalom ;* 11-14, David's sin and its punishment ; 15-20, the rebellion.
" 21-24, the *last years* of David's reign.

11.—I Kings.

The first and second books of Kings, like the two books of Samuel, were originally only one book in the Biblical Canon. The historical events range from David's death and Solomon's accession to the throne to the destruction of the kingdom of Judah. a period of about 400 years.

I Kings commences with the anointing of King Solomon and carries the history down to the death of King Jehoshaphat, 1000 to 900 B. C. Its 22 chapters may be divided into two equal parts, *viz.:*

Chapters 1-11, the *reign of Solomon.*
" 12-22, from the *division of the kingdom* to the death of Jehoshaphat.
(Chapters 17-22, principally the story of King Ahab and the prophet Elijah.)

12.—II Kings.

The second book continues the contemporary history of the two kingdoms of Judah and Israel to the downfall of both of them, comprising the period from 900 to 600 B. C. There are 25 chapters in this book, divided as follows, *viz.:*

Chapters 1–17, the contemporary *history of Judah and Israel;* 1–8, principally the ministry and the miracles of the prophet Elisha; 9–17, from the revolt of Jehu to the downfall of the kingdom of Israel.

" 18–25, the history of *Judah alone,* to the destruction of Jerusalem by Nebuchadnezzar.

13. —I Chronicles.

The two books of Chronicles contain a genealogical abstract of the whole of the sacred history down to the death of King Saul, and the reign of the subsequent kings of Judah to the Babylonish Captivity. While the books of Kings are written from the prophetical standpoint and give prominence to the kingdom of Israel, where Elijah and Elisha labored, the Chronicles are written from the levitical standpoint and the history of Judah only is given. In our English Bible the first book of Chronicles is divided into 29 chapters, (30 in the German).

Chapters 1–9, *mainly genealogies,* from Adam to the time of Ezra, after the Babylonish Captivity.

" 10–29, the *reign of King David;* 10–20, from the death of Saul to the completion of the victories of David; 21–29, David's political and religious administration.

14.—II Chronicles.

The second book contains the history of the kings of Judah, beginning with the reign of Solomon and ending with the edict of King Cyrus of Persia, at the close of the Babylonish Captivity. It covers the period from about 1000–536 B. C. The 36 chapters of II Chronicles, may be arranged in four groups of nine chapters each, *viz.:*
Chapters 1–9, the reign of King *Solomon.*
    "   10–18, from *Rehoboam* to *Jehoshaphat.*
    "   19–27, from *Jehoshaphat* to *Ahaz.*
    "   28–36, from *Ahaz* to *Zedekiah.*

15.—Ezra.

This book is a direct continuation of the second book of Chronicles and begins with a repetition of the last two verses of II Chronicles. It describes the return of the first colony with Zerubbabel, under King Cyrus, and of a second colony with Ezra, the scribe, under the reign of King Artaxerxes; a period of about 80 years, from 536–458 B. C. The rebuilding of the temple, and the purification of the people constitute the main topics of the book. Its 10 chapters, naturally, divide themselves into two parts, *viz. :*
Chapters 1–6, the *rebuilding* of the *temple*, under Zerubbabel.
    "   7–10, the *purification* of the *people,* under Ezra.

16.—Nehemiah.

A narrative of the commencement, progress and completion of the patriotic undertaking of Nehemiah to restore the city of Jerusalem, during the years from 445–433 B. C. The book has 13 chapters.

14

Chapters 1-7, the *rebuilding* of the *walls* and a list of the inhabitants of Jerusalem.

" 8-13, the *restoration* of the *Theocracy* and the re-dedication of the people to the service of Jehovah.

17.—Esther.

The writer of this book narrates, how a great danger which threatened the Hebrews living in the Persian empire was averted through the watchful care of Mordecai and of Queen Esther. If King Ahasuerus is the same person with Xerxes, the son of Darius Hystaspes, the time of this event may be fixed at 480 B. C. The 10 chapters of this book form two groups of equal length, *viz.:*

Chapters 1-5, the *danger.*

" 6-10, the *averting* of the danger.

II.—POETICAL BOOKS.

Under this head are comprehended Job, the Psalms, Proverbs, Ecclesiastes and the Song of Solomon. They are termed poetical, because they are generally composed of measured sentences and possess the characteristics of Hebrew poetry.

1. Job.

The object of this poem is to discuss the question: Why does God permit the righteous man to suffer? It solves this question by teaching men that realizing their own imperfection and ignorance, as well as the infinite wisdom and goodness of God, they must reject all confidence in their own merits, and with an humble faith submit to the divine decree. The book of Job has 42 chapters, and consists of five parts, *viz.:*

Chapters 1 and 2, the *historical introduction.*
"   3–31, the *discussion* between Job and his
        three friends, Eliphas, Bildad and
        Zophar; 3–14, the first discussion;
        15–21, the second discussion; 22–31,
        the third discussion.
"   32–37, the *speech of a fourth friend,*
        Elihu.
"   38–41, the *address* of *Jehovah.*
"   42, the *historical conclusion.*

2.—Psalms.

The collection of sacred hymns, composed by
David and other men of God down to the time of
the return from the Babylonish Captivity, contains
150 Psalms. Ancient tradition and internal evidence concur in separating them into five great
divisions or books. These books seem to have
been formed at different periods and differ in
their use of the divine names Jehovah (Lord)
and Elohim (God).

I. Psalms 1–41, composed by *David,* Jehovah
        psalms.
II.   "   42–72, composed by *David* and *Korah,*
        Elohim.
III. "   73–89, composed by *Asaph,* first part
        Elohim, later Jehovah.
IV.   "   90–106, one psalm of Moses, one of
        David, the *rest anonymous;* all
        Jehovah psalms.
V.   "   107–150, *all anonymous* and using the
        name of Jehovah ; later com-
        positions.

3.—Proverbs.

The book of Proverbs consists of short
discourses on various topics of religion and
morality, together with many pointed sayings
or maxims, expressing in few words lessons

of practical wisdom. It has 31 chapters. The following three divisions are distinctively marked:

Chapters 1-9, short *continuous discourses* on what constitutes true wisdom.

" 10-24, the *proverbs of Solomon*, mostly unconnected sayings.

" 25-31, proverbs collected by *Hezekiah* and later additions.

4.—Ecclesiastes.

Ecclesiastes signifies the preacher who addresses an assembly. It is the confession of a man of wide experience as to what the experiences of life have taught him. The 12 chapters which this book contains may be grouped, as follows:

Chapters 1-2, *a personal confession.*

" 3-5, the search after *happiness.*

" 6-8, the search after *wisdom.*

" 9-12, the *failure of both* and the lesson to be learned: "to fear God and keep His commandments."

5. —The Song of Solomon (Canticles).

This book, the plan and purpose of which are difficult to understand, seems to be a pastoral drama representing the victory of true love over temptations and trials. It is regarded as a symbol or allegory of the love which exists between Jehovah and His people. Its 8 chapters are variously divided into different acts or scenes, *e.g.:*

Chapters 1:2-2:7, the first meeting of Solomon and Sulamith.

" 2:8-3:5, Sulamith's separation from her beloved.

" 3:6-5:1, the bringing of the bride to Jerusalem.

"   5:2-8:4, Sulamith longing for her home.
"   8:5-8:14, Sulamith returns ; the victory
      of true love.

III.—PROPHETICAL BOOKS.

The prophets were inspired men sent or
appointed to make known the will of God both
with regard to their own time and with regard
to the future. Hence their writings are partly
doctrinal and partly predictive. Their personal
experiences also served as a testimony of God
to the people. There are 17 prophetical books
in the Old Testament.

I. - Isaiah.

The prophet Isaiah preached and prophesied
principally during the reign of the Kings Ahaz
and Hezekiah of Judah, from about 750 to 700 B.C.
The book of Isaiah consists of two distinct
parts, *viz.*, chapters 1 to 35 and chapters 40 to 66.
These two main parts are connected with each
other by four historical chapters, 36 to 39,
the contents of which, in a manner, seal the
discourses and prophecies of the first part and
introduce the prophetic panorama contained in
the second part.

Chapters 1–35, *discourses and prophecies* connected with *contemporaneous events*.
These may be subdivided into
three nearly equal groups, *viz.:*
1–12, discourses addressed to the
people of Israel in general ; 13–23,
"burdens" or prophecies addressed to the surrounding nations ; 24–35, discourses referring
to the reign of Hezekiah.

"   36–39, *historical ;* the invasion of the

Assyrians and the embassy from Babylon.

" 40-66, *a prophetic panorama of the future.* These 27 chapters are arranged in three groups of 9 chapters each. 40-48, the two contrasts, Jehovah and the idols, Israel and the heathen; 49-57, the present sufferings and the future glory of the servant of Jehovah ; 58-66, the nominal and the true church of God.

2. – Jeremiah.

Jeremiah, the tender-hearted and sorrowful prophet, who predicted and shared in the sufferings of the downfall of Judah and Jerusalem, bore witness by his own experiences as well as by his prophecies. His ministry, from about 630 to 590 B. C., became one long martyrdom. The book of Jeremiah, which contains alternately discourses and historical notes of the life of the prophet, does not appear to be arranged according to a regular plan or order. We may divide its 52 chapters, as follows :

Chapters 1-21, the *earlier ministry of the prophet* under Josiah and Jehoiakim.

" 22-31, additional *prophecies relating to the coming judgment.*

" 32-45, the *history* of the capture of Jerusalem.

" 46-52, prophecies against *foreign nations.*

3.—Lamentations.

Laments of the prophet Jeremiah over the exile of the people, the desolation of the land and the destruction of the temple. The five chapters of this book contain five elegies. Four of these have 22 verses each, according to the number of letters in the Hebrew alphabet; in the first, second and fourth each verse, in the Hebrew, begins with the corresponding letter; in the third each letter begins three verses in succession, making the total number of verses 66.

4.—Ezekiel.

Ezekiel, a prophet from the tribe of Levi, was carried to Babylon in the captivity of King Jeconiah of Judah and lived among the Jewish exiles in the land of the Chaldaeans, by whom he was held in high esteem. His call to the prophetic office took place in the 5th year of Jeconiah's captivity, 595 B. C. The book of Ezekiel contains 48 chapters and is divided into two equal parts, of which the destruction of Jerusalem is the turning point. The 24 chapters of the second part are again subdivided into two groups, one of 8, the other of 16 chapters.

Chapters 1–24, *denunciations* against Judah and Jerusalem, mingled with promises of mercy.

" 25–32, *prophecies against* seven *heathen nations.*

" 33–48, *promise of deliverance* and *of future glory* for Israel; 33–39, the victory over Gog ; 40-48, the vision of the new temple.

5.—Daniel.

Daniel, the fourth of " the greater prophets," a younger contemporary of Ezekiel and a fellow captive, but who was raised to a high political office, represented the cause of true religion at the court of the Babylonian and Medo-Persian kings. He seems to have prophesied between the years 590 and 535 B. C. The book of Daniel is divided into two equal parts, *viz.:*

Chapters 1-6, *historical* events.
    "   7-12, *apocalyptic ;* the future of the people of God and its relation to the powers of the world.

6.—Hosea.

'   ea heads the list of the "lesser prophets," although, as regards the chronological order, he probably holds the third place. His prophetic career extended from 785-725 B. C. He dwelt in the northern kingdom, that of Israel or Ephraim, and his prophecies principally regard that kingdom, then fast verging towards its ruin. His style of writing is abrupt and often obscure, but full of life and power. In the 14 chapters of the book, it is easy to recognize two great divisions, but the subdivison is difficult.

Chapters 1-3, the *prophet's marriage* with an unfaithful woman, a *symbol* of Israel's unfaithfulness over against Jehovah.
    "   4-14, *several discourses;* Jehovah pleads with Israel, his beloved but unfaithful spouse.

7.—Joel.

This prophet is supposed to have been the contemporary of Hosea. His commission was to Judah what that of Hosea was to the ten tribes ; his style is the very opposite of that of Hosea, very fluent and lucid. A public calamity of a twofold character: drought and a plague of locusts, forms the basis of the prophet's call to repentance. The three chapters of the book of Joel may be subdivided into two nearly equal parts, *viz.:*

Chapters 1:1–2:17, the *call to repentance.*
" 2:18–3:21, the *promise* of renewed mani-
festations of the divine favor.

8.—Amos.

Amos, originally a shepherd, was called by
God's spirit to be a prophet, although not trained
in a prophetic school. He traveled from Judah
into the northern kingdom and there exercised
his ministry, apparently not for any length of
time. His date may be fixed at 800 B. C. The
kingdom of Israel was then, under Jeroboam II,
at the height of power and luxury ; the prophet
was sent as a herald of the coming judgment.
The book of Amos contains 9 chapters, which
may be arranged as follows:
Chapters 1–3, the *judgment* impending upon the
nations generally.
" 4–6, the *judgment* upon the *northern kingdom,* in particular.
" 7–9, *symbolical visions.*

9. –Obadiah.

It is probable that Obadiah was a contemporary
with Jeremiah, living about 600 B. C. The inser-
tion of his prophecy between those of Amos and
Jonah is explained on the ground of its being an
amplification of the last five verses of Amos.
The book of Obadiah which contains but one
chapter denounces judgments on the Edomites
and promises restoration and future prosperity
to Israel.

10.–Jonah.

The general opinion is that Jonah was the first
of the prophets whose writings have been preserved and that his time dates between 850 and

800 B. C. The book of Jonah is chiefly historical. It contains an account of the prophet's mission to the city of Nineveh, in four chapters.

Chapters 1 and 2, Jonah's flight and return.

" 3 and 4, Jonah's preaching and the re- mission of the judgment.

11.—Micah.

Micah exercised the prophetical office during the reigns of Jotham, Ahaz and Hezekiah, kings of Judah, that is between the years 750 and 700 B. C. He was, therefore, the contemporary of the prophet Isaiah and resembles him in the clear, concise and poetical style of his writings. The 7 chapters of the book of Micah are divided into three parts, each commencing with "Hear ye."

Chapters 1 and 2, *addressed to all the people,* de- scribe the coming judgment.

" 3-5, the judgment upon *the leaders* of the people, and the coming of Messiah.

" 6 and 7, *Jehovah's argument* with Israel.

12.—Nahum.

The date of Nahum can not be accurately determined, but it is probable that he flourished in the latter half of the reign of Hezekiah, and wrote his prophecy soon after the destruction of Samaria by the Assyrians, about 720 B. C. The subject of the prophecy is simply "the burden of Nineveh," a continuation or supplement to Jonah. The book of Nahum has three chapters.

Chapter 1, the judgment is *coming.*

" 2, the judgment is *accomplished.*

" 3, the judgment is *reviewed.*

13.—Habakkuk.

The position of this prophecy in the Old Testament canon, as well as internal evidence, lead us to the conclusion, that Habakkuk was a contemporary of the prophet Jeremiah, 625 B. C. As Nahum had declared the coming judgment upon the Assyrians, so Habakkuk was commissioned to denounce the judgment against the Chaldeans. His style is peculiarly grand and sublime. The three chapters of Habakkuk may be analyzed as follows:

Chapter 1, the *Chaldeans* are *instruments* of God in bringing judgment.
" 2, they are in turn *judged themselves.*
" 3, the *prayer* of the prophet.

14.—Zephaniah.

Zephaniah, according to the inscription of his book, was another contemporary of Jeremiah, and prophesied under the reign of King Josiah, 625 B. C. His writings are characterized chiefly by the harmony of the composition and the gracefulness of the style. The three chapters of Zephaniah, like those of Nahum and Habakkuk, contain a declaration of judgment over Judah and Jerusalem, mingled with promises of a future restoration.

Chapter 1, the *judgment against Judah.*
" 2, the judgment against *Judah's enemies.*
" 3, *Jerusalem,* though now under discipline, shall be *restored.*

15.—Haggai.

The remaining three of the minor prophets, *viz.:* Haggai, Zechariah and Malachi, flourished after the return from the Babylonish Captivity. Haggai was raised up by the Lord, about 520 B. C., for the purpose of stimulating Zerubbabel and the people to resume the building of the temple which had been interrupted. The two chapters of the book of Haggai seem to be but an outline or summary of the discourses of this prophet.

Chapter 1, the discourse delivered in the sixth month.
" 2, discourses delivered in the seventh and ninth months.

16.—Zechariah.

Zechariah was the younger contemporary of Haggai (about 500 B. C.), and was called to the prophetic office for the same purpose, *viz.:* the rebuilding of the temple. Like Jeremiah and Ezekiel before him, he was priest as well as prophet. The book of Zechariah contains 14 chapters, and, like the book of Isaiah, it is divided into two main parts, of six chapters each, with a practical discourse in two chapters, as a connecting link between the first and second part.

Chapters 1-6, a *series of visions*, descriptive of those hopes of which the building of the temple was the foundation. (1, the rider in the valley of myrtles ; 2, the four horns ; 3, the high priest Joshua ; 4, the candlestick ; 5, the flying roll ; 6, the four chariots.)
" 7-8, a *discourse* on true religion and a promise of the restoration of Israel.
" 9-14, a *prophetic panorama* including the times of the Messiah, and the restoration of Israel and Jerusalem subdivided into two burdens ; 9-11, the coming of the

Messiah and His rejection; 12–14, the repentance of Israel and its final glory.

17.—Malachi.

Malachi, the last of the prophets, completed the canon of the Old Testament Scriptures after the second·return of Nehemiah from Persia, about 420 B. C. He occupied the same position with regard to the reformation under Nehemiah, which Isaiah held in the time of Hezekiah.

The four chapters of Malachi may be grouped as follows:

Chapters 1 and 2, *reproof* of the sins of the people.
" 3 and 4, the *Lord's coming*, to bring judgment and salvation.

B.—THE NEW TESTAMENT.

The New Testament contains 27 books, 5 of which are historical, 21 doctrinal and 1 prophetical.

I.—HISTORICAL BOOKS.

The historical books of the New Testament comprise the four Gospels, (*i.e.*, a fourfold account of the earthly life and work of our Saviour,) and the book of Acts, the latter being a brief record of the Christian Church, from its founding to the imprisonment of St. Paul in Rome, A. D. 63.

The first three Gospels are termed the synoptical Gospels, because, as regards their contents and general character, they proceed upon a common outline. The narration of events, with the exception of the last journey to Jerusalem, is confined to Christ's working in Galilee, and is a simple statement of facts, while St. John's Gospel refers more fully to Christ's working in Judea, with an occasional comment by the writer. The synoptical Gospels refer mainly to Christ's *work*, and to the establishment of His kingdom on earth, that of John refers rather to the *person* of Christ and the eternal decrees of God. Matthew, Mark and Luke represent Christ principally as the Son of man, the Messiah and the Saviour, the fourth Gospel represents Him, first of all, as the eternal Son of God, the only mediator between God and men.

1.—Matthew.

The first Gospel was written by Matthew, surnamed Levi, one of the twelve apostles, but formerly a publican or tax-gatherer. It was intended primarily for the Hebrews and for Jewish-Christian converts. Hence the frequent quotations from the Old Testament, the tracing of Christ's genealogy to Abraham, etc. The writer represents Christ as the Messiah of Israel, the new lawgiver, the true prophet, priest and king. The Gospel according to Matthew contains 28 chapters, which may be arranged in four groups of seven chapters each:

Chapters 1-7, the *beginning of Christ's ministry*, including the "Sermon on the Mount."
"   8-14, His *glorious work* in Galilee.
"   15-21, the steadily increasing *opposition* of His enemies.
"   22-28, His *last discourses*, *death* and *resurrection*.

2.—Mark.

The second Gospel, composed by Mark, the
assistant of the apostle Peter, seems to have
been written principally for the Romans. It
records the deeds rather than the words of
Christ, and represents Him as the powerful ·
worker of miracles. The narrative seems to
follow the strict chronological order of events.
The 16 chapters of this Gospel are divided into
two nearly equal parts, *viz.:*

Chapters 1–19, Christ's ministry in *Galilee.*
" 10–16, His ministry in *Peraea* and *Judea,*
including His death and resur-
rection.

3. – Luke.

Luke, the companion of St. Paul, the apostle
of the Gentiles, and himself of Gentile birth,
wrote his Gospel especially for the Greeks.
Christ is to him, above all, the ideal man, the
Saviour of all men, the friend of sinners and the
Redeemer of the world. Luke wrote after a
careful examination of the existing records and
sources of the Gospel narrative, and arranged
his story according to a systematic plan. The
24 chapters of Luke's Gospel may be arranged
in four groups, of 3, 6, 9 and again 6 chapters,
respectively.

Chapters 1–3, the *preparation* for Christ's ministry.
" 4–9, *discourses* and *acts* of our Lord,
belonging to *Capernaum* and
neighborhood, recorded also by
Matthew and Mark.
" 10–18, a collection of *accounts*, referring
to "Christ's journey," mostly
peculiar to *Luke.*

"   19-24, the story of Christ's *sufferings* and *triumph*.

4.– John.

The apostle John, doubtless, wrote his Gospel narrative some time after the other three Gospels had been written, perhaps about A. D. 75, and principally for Christian readers. It supplements the other gospels in that it contains some important events and especially discourses, not recorded in them; but it has its own scope, character and purpose. The apostle after stating dogmatically that Jesus Christ was the incarnate Word, the son of God, proves this statement by the words and works of Christ which convinced even the doubting Thomas. St. John relates but nine of the miracles of Christ. His Gospel, like that of Mark, is arranged chronologically. It contains 21 chapters.

Chapter 1:1–18, the *dogmatical* statement.
"   1:19–20:29, the *historical* proof; 1:19–11: 57, Christ's ministry; 12:1–20:29, His sufferings and triumph.
"   21:1–25, the *conclusion*.

5.—The Acts.

The Acts of the Apostles, a second treatise by the author of the third Gospel, may have been written about A. D. 65; at least the period comprised in its pages terminates in the year 63 A. D. The book contains principally the acts of Peter and Paul, the former being the central figure of the first group and the latter of the second group. We divide the 28 chapters of the Acts into 4 parts of 7 chapters each:

Chapters 1–7, the Church in *Jerusalem*, A. D. 31–37.

"   8-14, the *spread of the Gospel*: Paul's
        first missionary journey through
        Asia Minor, A. D. 37-50.
"   15-21, the *second and third Missionary
        journey* of Paul, A. D. 50-58.
"   22-28, *Paul a prisoner* and his journey to
        Rome, A. D. 58-63.

II.—THE EPISTLES.

Of the 21 Epistles contained in the New
Testament two-thirds, *viz*.: 13 or 14 are St.
Paul's, the remaining third is from the pen of
other apostles or of men having apostolic
authority. St. Paul's epistles are not arranged
chronologically, but according to their contents.
In the order of the time of writing the two
epistles to the Thessalonians come first; a
second group comprises Romans, Corinthians
and Galatians; a third group Ephesians, Colossians, Philippians and Philemon; and the fourth
group the epistles to Timothy and Titus.

1.—Romans.

The epistle to the Romans was written at
Corinth, during the third missionary journey of
Paul, A. D. 58. The church at Rome was not
founded by an apostle, but by Christian converts
from the East; it included Jewish Christians and
Gentile Christians. This epistle stands first in
the order of Paul's epistles because of the
importance of the church addressed, and the
importance of its contents. The subject is:
"The Gospel of Jesus Christ the salvation both
of the Jews and of the Gentiles." The 16
chapters into which the epistle is divided, group
themselves as follows:

Chapters 1-11, the *doctrinal part.*
" 	a. 1-8, the *Gospel of Christ is the salvation of individual men.* 1-4, on what the Gospel is founded, *viz.:* the general need of a Saviour (1: 18-3:20), and the divine promises (3:21-4 end); 5-8, what the Gospel does for the believer, *viz.:* it justifies (5), sanctifies (6 and 7), and it glorifies (8).
" 	b. 9-11, the *Gospel of Christ* is the *salvation of Jews and Gentiles* as a whole; 9, the mystery of Israel's rejection; 10, the explanation; 11, the final solution.
" 	12-16, *the practical part;* lessons derived from the doctrinal part; 12 and 13, Individual Christian conduct ; 14 and 15, Christian fellowship and social relations; 16, greetings and commendations.

2.—I Corinthians.

The first epistle to the Corinthians was written during the apostle's three years' sojourn in the city of Ephesus, about A. D. 57, one year before he wrote to the Romans. The letter was called forth by the information which Paul had received of divisions that existed in the Corinthian church, of sins having occurred among Christian converts and of questions that had arisen concerning matters of Christian practice. The general subject of the epistle is: "The Christian Congregation, its doctrine and ritual," but the contents are extremely varied. We may group the 16 chapters as follows:

Chapters 1-4, *their dissensions* contrasted with the spirit of Christ and of His apostles.

" 5-10, *social relations* (Christian discipline, going to law, marriage,
giving and taking offense).
" 11-14, public *worship and spiritual
gifts.*
" 15 and 16, the *resurrection of the dead*
and miscellaneous matters.

3.—II Corinthians.

The second epistle was sent a few months
subsequent to the first (A. D. 58) from Macedonia.
It was occasioned by the information which the
apostle had received with regard to the effect of
the first letter. The majority of the members of
the church had heeded Paul's admonitions, a
minority opposed him and doubted his authority.
Hence this second epistle relates mainly to the
person and work of the apostle Paul. It has 13
chapters.

Chapters 1-7, the *position and work of Paul* and
his relation to his converts.
" 8-9, directions about *collections* for the
church in Jerusalem,
" 10-13, defense of the *apostolic character*
of Paul.

4.—Galatians.

The date of this epistle is earlier than either
Romans or Corinthians, perhaps A. D. 55. It
was addressed to the churches of the Asiatic
province of Galatia, which had been founded
by the apostle during his second Missionary
journey, A. D. 51. The letter appears to have
been called forth hy the information that certain
Jewish Christians urged the necessity of observ-
ing the Mosaic law, circumcision, etc. The
theme is: The law and the Gospel.

Chapters 1 and 2, *apologetic;* a *vindication* of Paul
　　　and his doctrine.
　" 　3 and 4, *polemical ;* a *series of proofs*
　　　drawn from the Old Testament,
　　　that the law was fulfilled in
　　　Christ.
　" 　5 and 6, *practical;* inferences from the
　　　foregoing discussion.

5.—Ephesians.

This letter was written by Paul, while he was
a prisoner at Rome, presumably immediately
after he had written the epistle to the Colossians,
perhaps in the early part of A. D. 62. It was
addressed to the church at Ephesus, where he
abode so long, and from the elders of which
he parted with such an affectionate farewell.
Ephesus was the city in which stood the famous
temple of Diana. Probably with reference to
that temple the apostle, in this epistle, treats of
the spiritual temple of the Church of Christ.

The six chapters of the epistle naturally divide
themselves into two portions:

Chapters 1-3, *doctrinal;* the spiritual foundation,
　　　the glory and the aim of the Church
　　　of Christ.
　" 　4-6, *hortatory* and *practical;* what spirit
　　　must pervade the Church and its
　　　members, individually and collec-
　　　tively.

6.—Philippians.

The Christian community at Philippi distin-
guished itself by its liberality. They contributed
readily to the collection made for the relief of
the poor in Jerusalem; they entertained the
apostle on his several visits to the city with an
affectionate cordiality, and after Paul's arrival in

Rome, they sent Epaphroditus to him with supplies and to render him service. Hence the epistle addressed to the Philippians. which was written from Rome about A. D. 63, is particularly full of brotherly affection and good wishes. It is altogether a practical epistle. The contents of the four chapters may be classified as follows:

Chapter 1, *information* respecting himself.

" 2 and 3, *good advice* to his Christian converts.

" 4, *acknowledgment* of their kindness.

7.—Colossians.

This epistle, chronologically considered, seems to have preceded those to the Ephesians and Philippians. Its date of writing is the early portion of Paul's captivity at Rome, A. D. 61 or 62. It was called forth by information received from Epaphras and Onesimus, and designed to warn the Christians at Colossae, against certain false teachers, whose teaching tended to obscure the eternal glory and dignity of Christ. The epistle contains four chapters and is divided into two equal parts:

Chapters 1 and 2, *doctrinal part:* 1, Christ the only mediator of salvation ; 2, warning against false philosophy and ceremonial legalism.

" 3 and 4, *practical part:* Christian duties.

8.—I Thessalonians.

The two epistles addressed to the Thessalonians are the earliest of Paul's epistles. They were written from Corinth, not long after the apostle had founded the church at Thessalonica, probably A. D. 52. One of their special features is the instruction which the apostle imparts, concerning

the second coming of the Lord. I Thessalonians
is divided into five chapters, which may be
arranged in two parts, each closing with a prayer.

Chapters 1–3, *narrative portion;* their conversion,
Paul's ministry among them, and
his concern for them.

" 4–5, *hortatory portion;* Christian conduct
and the coming of the Lord.

9.—II Thessalonians.

The contents of this epistle show it to have
been written very soon after the former one and
at the same place. Its leading motive appears
to be the desire of correcting certain errors and
misrepresentations, especially with regard to
the second advent of Christ. The subject and
general character are the same as in the first
epistle; also the division into two parts, each
closing with a prayer.

Chapters 1 and 2, *doctrinal part;* encouragement
under persecutions, and in-
struction concerning the Anti-
christ.

" 3, *practical part;* exhortation to
prayer and reproof of the dis-
orderly.

10.— I Timothy.

The date of the two epistles to Timothy and
of the epistle to Titus has been a subject of
much controversy, some assigning them to the
years A. D. 56–58, and others to the last years of
the life of the apostle, after his release from the
first imprisonment at Rome. According to the
latter view they were written after A. D, 63.
They differ, in character, from the preceding
epistles, in that they are not addressed to con-
gregations, but to ministers of the Church, and

speak particularly of the qualifications and duties of the Christian ministry.

The first epistle to Timothy is divided into 6 chapters. These may be grouped in two equal parts, although it is hardly possible to discern any regular order or connection of thought.

Chapters 1–3, *the principles.* with regard to Christian doctrine (1), religious worship (2) and holy orders (3).

" 4–6, *the application* of the principles; Timothy's personal conduct (4), his pastoral duties (5) and his ministerial work in general (6).

11.—II Timothy.

The second epistle is perhaps the last letter of the apostle Paul that has been preserved. It consists of 4 chapters, the contents of which may be arranged as follows:

Chapters 1 and 2, the *present duties* of Timothy; to develop his gifts, to be courageous and firm.

" 3 and 4, the *outlook* into the *future;* what Timothy must prepare for and what Paul has in expectation.

12.—Titus.

Titus, a gentile Christian, converted through Paul's instrumentality and afterwards his fellow worker, was left by the apostle on the island of Crete to organize the churches there by appointing presbyters in every city, The epistle is supposed to have been written after the first epistle to Timothy. It contains directions how to discharge the duties of one who is set over the churches. The tone is more official, while in the epistles to Timothy it is confidential. The three chapters into which the epistle is divided may be analyzed thus:

Chapter 1, church *government.*

" 2, *doctrine and pastoral work.*

" 3, *discipline.*

13.—Philemon.

This is a letter of recommendation, addressed to a member of the church at Colossae, in behalf of a slave, Onesimus by name, who having fled from his master's service to the city of Rome, was converted under Paul's ministry to the Christian faith. and then sent back to his master. It was, probably, written and delivered at the same time with the epistle to the Colossians. The tenderness and delicacy of this epistle, together with the skill of its composition, have always been greatly admired.

14.—Hebrews.

Whether this epistle was written by the apostle Paul or some one else, is a question which can not be fully decided. If written by Paul, it is supposed to date from the end of his first captivity in Rome about A. D. 63. It was, probably, addressed to the Jews in Jerusalem and Palestine. Its general theme is: "Christ and the new covenant superior to the old dispensation." It is divided into 13 chapters which group themselves in three parts of 4 chapters each, with the 13th chapter as a conclusion.

Chapters 1-4, *Christ the best Mediator* of revelation; 1 and 2, superior to prophets and angels; 3 and 4, superior to Moses, Joshua and Aaron.

" 5-8, *Christ the great priest-king,* like Melchizedek; 5 and 6, appointed of God and before whom every knee must bow; 7 and 8, a true highpriest.

" 9-12, the *new covenant superior* to the old ; 9 and 10, it brings us into true communion with God; 11 and 12, patterns of holy living, in the faithful men of old, must be imitated.

15.—James.

The writer of the epistle was probably James, surnamed the Just, the first "bishop" of the Church in Jerusalem, who is identified with the apostle James, the less, or with the " brother of the Lord." The time of writing is not known. It is addressed to Jewish Christians and its object appears not to be to teach doctrine, but to exhort his readers to patience under manifold trials, and to warn them against a form of religion which is devoid of the true spirit.

Chapter 1 teaches the *Christian conduct under trials.*

" 2-4 *warn against various sins* to which Jewish Christians were most liable.

" 5 *exhorts* them to be honest, patient and prayerful.

16.—I Peter.

This epistle appears to have been written at Babylon, where the Christian religion was established at an early date and where the apostle Peter appears to have resided for some time. It was addressed to the churches in Asia Minor and is supposed to have been written, after the apostle had seen and studied some of the writings of St. Paul, probably not before A. D. 63. It is mainly a practical epistle intended to strengthen the believers and to exhort them to walk worthily of their profession. While St. Paul dwells especially upon saving faith, St. Peter's special theme is the glorious hope of the Christian. The 5 chapters of this first epistle may be arranged, as follows:

Chapter 1, what Christians have *received*.
" 2 and 3, how, accordingly, they *should live*.
" 4 and 5, what they shall *strive after*, especially in view of the future manifestation of Christ.

17.—II Peter.

The second epistle of Peter was addressed to the same persons as the former one, and must have been written shortly before the martyrdom of the apostle. It includes a passage which bears a strong resemblance to the epistle of Jude, which Peter may have read. The three chapters, into which this Epistle is divided, may be said to refer, respectively, to the past, present and future.

Chapter 1, *the past*, the sure foundation.
" 2, *the present*, the dangers which beset their path.
" 3, *the future*, the coming of the Lord.

18.—I John.

From the patriarchal tone of this epistle it is inferred that It was written, when the apostle John was advanced in age, about A. D. 90, and perhaps from Ephesus, where the apostle ordinarily resided. In the introduction St. John states, as the purpose of the epistle: to declare the Word of life, in order that he and his readers may have true communion with God in Christ, and with each other. St. John is the apostle of *love*, but this love springs from faith and produces obedience. The five chapters of this first epistle may be arranged under the following heads :

Chapters 1 and 2, *God is light;* we must come to the light, confess our sins, be cleansed from sin and living in communion with God, must walk in the light.

" 3 and 4, *God is love;* the children of God love and obey their father, and love the brethren.

" 5, the faith, love and obedience of the children of God *overcome* the world.

19.—II John.

This short epistle is addressed to a Christian lady, whom the apostle desires to warn against the preachers of a doctrine, which is not in accordance with the love of Christ.

20.—III John.

In this epistle the apostle commends to a certain Cajus, some brethren, perhaps evangelists, who were strangers in the place where he lived. A certain Diotrephes had used his influence against receiving such missionary brethren.

21.—Jude.

From early times this epistle has been attributed to Jude, "the bishop of Jerusalem." Its object is to warn Christian readers against ungodly men, "who turn the grace of our God into lasciviousness." The writer describes, forcibly, the character and the punishment of such men.

III.—PROPHETICAL BOOKS.

The New Testament contains but one prophetical book, properly so called, although there are

many prophetical passages in the discourses of
our Lord and in the Epistles.

22.—Revelation.

The book of Revelation was probably the last
book which the apostle John wrote; according
to the church-father Irenæus "towards the close
of the reign of the Emperor Domitian," that is
about A. D. 95–97. Tradition says, that in the
persecution under Domitian, John was banished
to the island of Patmos. The 22 chapters into
which the book of Revelation is divided, naturally, group themselves in two equal parts.

Chapters 1–11, *the world's history, from the time
of the apostle to the end;* 1–3, first
vision: the Son of man and the
church, or the seven epistles to
the seven churches; 4–7, second
vision, the Lamb and the seven
seals, or the riddles of the world's
history solved by Christ; 8–11
third vision, the seven trumpets
and seven thunders, or the divine judgments and the victo-
rious establishment of Christ's
kingdom.

Chapters 12–22, the *assaults* of the devil and his
agents *upon the Church, and their
final destruction;* 12–14, the war
between Christ and the Anti-
christ; the child and the dragon
(12), the church and the beast
(13), Zion and Babylon (14); 15–19,
the judgments upon Babylon
and the beast; the seven vials of
of wrath (15 and 16), Babylon and
the beast destroyed (17-19); 20-22,
the end of the world and the new
Jerusalem.